CITY *of* REGRET

CITY *of* REGRET
ANDREW KOZMA

ZONE 3 PRESS
Clarksville, Tennessee

ZONE 3 PRESS
Clarksville, Tennessee

LCCN: 2007926061
ISBN: 978-0-9786127-1-9

Cover and book design by ***David Bieloh***
Cover Art: Untitled monotype image by ***Ron Buffington***

A Tennessee Board of Regents Institution

Austin Peay State University is an equal opportunity
employer committed to the education of a nonracially
identifiable student body. AP012/07-07/Thomson-
Shore/Dexter, MI

ACKNOWLEDGEMENTS

I would like to gratefully acknowledge the magazines and editors that published the following poems, some in slightly different forms:

American Letters & Commentary: "Sword of Damascus"

Best New Poets 2005: "Too Steep to Climb"

Borderlands: Texas Poetry Review: "Mary Fights the Memories of Her Tongue" (as "Mary")

Broken Bridge Review: "'Confess,' you'd said, asleep"

Caketrain: "After the Cremation," "Meanings," and "The Funeral"

Cimarron Review: "The Cleansing Power of Metaphor" and "One of the Unburied Dead"

Clackamas Literary Review: "The Nuns Remove Their Noses and Lips"

Forklift, Ohio: "Dream of Small Things"

The GSU Review: "Through Ice"

Lilies and Cannonballs Review: "Blood Perimeter" and "Promises"

Paper Street: "Her Lover, Gone to Buy a Drink, Perhaps"

Pebble Lake Review: "Acropolis," "Another Poem on Red," and "Dedicatory Letter"

Post Road: "Invader" and "What Is"

Puerto del Sol: "Dis"

The Texas Review: "The Cremation"

Washington Square: "Limits to Science and Medicine"

Willow Springs: "Quarantine"

Zone 3: "Reclamation"

Three mentors have been crucial to the writing of this book, through careful attention to individual poems and advice about poetry in general: Adam Zagajewski, Sidney Wade, and, especially, William Logan.

Though half of these poems were written elsewhere, the large community of writers at the University of Houston, both students and teachers, has been instrumental in the development of this book. I want to single out as attentive readers and supportive friends David Ray Vance, Kwang Lee, Sasha West, Kelly Moore, Ranjana Varghese, and, finally, Jericho Brown, who inspired the final form of the book.

I also want to thank all those who provided emotional support, friendship, and distraction from the problems of the day, especially Erin, Kara, Jason, Bryan, Brendan, Heather, Tamara, Laura E., Laura C., and the staff at Empire Cafe.

Thanks and love to my mom, brother, and sister-in-law who push me forward when I'd rather stay where I am. Though the journey is difficult, I always find myself in a better place.

CONTENTS

Introduction

WALLS MERGING WITH AIR

Style, said Henry James, is the means by which "we shall be saved." Andrew Kozma's *City of Regret,* a kind of odyssey into classical Dis through the medium of a modernist language that experiments with sudden associations and turns, strives toward just such a salvation. The odyssey is one that uses Greece as an anchoring point from which to voyage over a number of concerns, most prominently the death of the speaker's father which acts as a tonal backdrop for the entire book. Moving adroitly between settings, states of mind, between vision and sight, this is a poetry that is cinematic in its changes of mood, texture, and color, allowing the reader multiple perspectives. Indeed, the speaker himself is part Odysseus exploring our conscious world, part Orpheus bringing us news from the underworld and the unconscious.

It is no surprise, then, that the poetry takes what Roethke called "desperate leaps" and links, by which he meant a language that reveals the depth and intensity of our emotional life. "Agoraphobia," for example, is worth quoting entire:

> Look up and a nutshell carves itself into the sky,
> wormholes draining light
> like a car dripping oil. Under this coffee-shop roof,
>
> surrounded by glass and the pop
> of empty air, concrete is quicksand.
> But your hand lies there
>
> like a painted anchor, a string of fishhooks
> dulled with wear,
> a twin I cannot name, a gag,

a one-way mirror, a mannequin
on a thin lattice of steel, a trellis
for thorns, a cupped nest,

there, on your side of the table, prepared.
A mug steams between us
like a wall merging with air.

    The opening line surprises by its reversal of the more
traditional rhetorical form that would have the sky looking like the
inside of a nutshell. But that perspective is suddenly shifted with
the mention of the wormholes (literal as far as the shell goes, and
scientifically theoretical as far as the sky goes), and further shifted
with the image of the "car dripping oil." All that is an associatively
original complex (sky-nutshell-oil pan), but it goes further when
we realize that the complex is a metaphor for the "coffee-shop
roof." Now the image of the nutshell also leans a bit towards the
literal ceiling texture, and the oil drip starts to figure as the coffee
drip. In a few lines we are both confined and wanting to burst out.
It is in this context that the "characters" come into focus. The
simile for the other's hand starts another series of connections—an
"anchor" and "a string of fishhooks" give way to the more visceral
"gag," but also emerging is this (feared) "twin I cannot name" who
may be merely the speaker's own reflection in a "one-way mirror"
that has, in a sense, "hooked" him. But then the speaker/other is
also a "mannequin" enclosed by the trellis/lattice/nest images. As
often happens in Kozma's poems, the last few lines act as a kind of
Shakespearean couplet tying everything together. Dramatically, the
speaker has been caught in a public place, a coffee shop, and he
spies himself in a mirror where he first thinks the reflection is a
dreaded other person, thus intensifying the agoraphobia. The last
two lines then assert a wall between self/other self, but a wall that
is undergoing a gradual dissolution so that the final fear is a fear of
the self.

Of course, the poem can be read another way, depending on how literally or figuratively we take the language. Is the twin a distinct other? Is the mannequin an image for the impersonality of the other, the lack of selfhood in the self? An ideal from the perspective of an agoraphobic? All of these? Is the speaker literally outside imagining himself in a confined place? Is the nutshell on the table in front of him? And is it an image for what he'd like to be—shelled? It is the richness of Kozma's language that opens up these possibilities to exist as if we were experiencing several planes of reality at once. In "Promises," for instance, the speaker focuses on a "granite bench... scored like limestone" and realizes that there is another level of reality present:

> Parts of us are still there, worn into stone,
> a thread of your green skirt, blood
> from a scraped knuckle. It's these memories
> singing ever deeper.

Once we begin to understand objects as containing what our experiences, vision, and history invest in them, they become "deeper." As a result, not only objects but we ourselves are changed, defined by what is invisible, beyond the physical. So the poem ends:

> Your face, the slope
> of your nose, becomes the rosary that wears
> with prayer, that shines with disappearance.

Despite the poems' attempts to create alternate worlds that might save us, there is always the pressure of the present world, the world of "disappearances" that gives Kozma's work an elegiac tone. It is this tone that keeps reminding us, in the face of the losses, the deaths, the departures that fill the book, that it is poetry's endless struggle to work against these things despite the odds.

In a poetry of such provisional interpenetrations perhaps the ultimate question is provided in "Limits to Science and Medicine," that is, "how love is filtered into the body." In that poem, which starts with a literal opening of the body, the image of a flock of birds crossing a highway is related to "thousands / of dark arrowheads" and a potential "suture for the sky," both the instrument of wounding and of healing. That the body is figured as both highway and sky further suggests how much this poet looks beyond the literal world. The poem ends with what might be taken as a coda for the whole book, for the process of creation and revaluation, observation and sudden discovery, the stuff, that is, of true vision:

What does it mean

to be completely understood, to have an eye
that comprehends the inside, that follows the light
digested by the nerve, makes of it a manual for the world?

Hold yourself like a string. Realize what it means
to hold a stone, and that if there were a door
in the stone we could disassemble the hinges.

Richard Jackson
University of Tennessee at Chattanooga

And now with sudden swift emergence
Come the women in dark glasses and the humpbacked surgeons
And the scissor man.
　　　　　　　　　　　　–W. H. Auden, "The Summer holds: upon its
　　　　　　　　　　　　　　　　glittering lake"

DIS

My father said I would not find him here,
but I've 2 coins for passage, 3 boiled ox bones, 1 cup blood.
Hell is a room the size of the world:

I've been two days on the Plain of Needles, each one sewing
some poor soul to the landscape. The souls exhale sin
with every breath, growing thinner

until pale flowers push through their skin toward the sky
and an imagined Heaven. I pick a flower,
and grind the petals between my teeth.

The distance holds Dis, the city of regret. The way back
is blocked by frogs with human eyes in their mouths,
but there's no danger if you don't stare.

Some figure beckons—but it is only a shadow
shorn by the dimming sun. The sun is fed
more bodies and wells into brightness

like a picked scab—it has followed me, bobbing
on its giant stalk, leering so close
when I cleansed myself in the River of Unshed Tears

that burning eyelashes hallowed the ground like snow.
An angel on the hill ahead is slowly devouring his legs.
When I reach him he is gone; the city has snuck up; it's a bully.

Its stone walls are dust beneath my fingers. I breathe in,
let my lungs calcify. My words emerge
under slabs of rock. The city is empty and falling,

the wide courtyards now full of eyeless cats.
When a ravine splits the sky, Earth's muddy light
unearths my father. *We have much to talk about.*

ENTRANCES

THE CLEANSING POWER OF METAPHOR

*[Her] body that was now only a device for the
production of pain...*
                                    ~Jean Thompson, "Mother Nature"

A portrait of my father in this sterile room:
Gulliver staked by the Lilliputians, pierced
by the spokesman's constant buzz; a fragile glass
spider waiting in its web, organs visible and aerating;

a snarl of spaghetti entrenched in sauce;
a maze of overpasses, cloverleafs, turnabouts,
HOV lanes, on-ramps, accidents at all the exits;
a hibernation of snakes; a full switchboard

humming with the shards of voices;
the burning Hindenburg tangled in its skeleton;
a man descending into dark water, his face
cupped with tension; a drawing scribbled through.

NIGHT MEETING

The sun embeds itself in the horizon.
Streetlamps turn surfaces shiny

with a thin sugar glaze.
I stumble on a dead squirrel

mid-street, face curious,
body split open.

The fur pulses with ants
who line the skin like stitches.

THE TRANSPLANT WARD

Even the most sincere in need
wait months or years, eyes fixed

to the walls like water stains.
They practice feeling hollow

with hands on their chests,
caging those small moments of space

they won't remember
when surgeons unhook the heart

and hold the body open
as it rushes to fill itself.

THAT WE MAY FIND OURSELVES AT DEATH

When you are late for death, where do you go instead?
Those nights I thought I was finally dreaming,
the TV interfered so my father failed to whisper in my ear.

How do you confront what is already gone?
The sky above blackens with the absence of jets.
I remember the Acropolis: shattered

with puddles; the horizon the light blue of ice
edging a pond; the sky clouded as though the stone
itself were evaporating. Does the body transcend

the earth as details transcend memory? Someone walked
with me up the path, to the edge of the hill, and looked,
as well, on the ash-fogged streets. Who is it

that also knows what I saw crawling through Athens
leaving flame in its wake? Does she remember our room
an oven? If we had known, would we have made love?

Would the clouds have come down to greet us?
That time was death's time. We had not known it.

Through Ice

"What is this? Can it be that it is Death?" And the
inner voice answered: "Yes, it is Death."
                    ~Leo Tolstoy, "The Death of Ivan Ilyich"

Those moments when knowledge orients and shuttles
in one direction, we ourselves stall. As at a hotel bar, dignified
dollars smoothed into condensation,
and the spotted glasses cramped above my head,
dislocating. The bartender says nothing
but I imagine the conversation didactic: *You bleed to think? Risky*
is the rest. Curry to sear your parent's breath.
Those moments air becomes solid and you stare through ice
like a man in a glacier. Image recedes.
Outside, in the rain, on a corner, is a love,
my love, waiting for a cab to enclose her,
or someone very like a cab. And the street is like slate,
and the rain is like bullets, and the sun, in the blue sky,
is like transformation explaining photographs
of what it was. Those moments I feel a paper cut,
how the skin can be whole and divided at once.
I have explained the states of matter and witnessed students
understand, suddenly filtered into knowing.

THE VISION OF ST. JEROME

Jerome is unsurprised. His gray clothes and skin differ
only by a line and, on his knees, his fingers grasp
dirt the color of his thigh, but he is not surprised.
Circling him are the pale shadows of vultures
invisible against the sky, hidden like the birds
that break his morning open. He breathes silence.

Or a hum, the gray, dirtied air,
a murmuring that entreats him to forget
completely the stiff bed where he rests
with his eyes open to the lacerated ceiling,
the weight of his shriveled muscles, the writhing hunger,
and recognize the blurred lines of this gray world.

Here, rhymes deciphered in nature and salvation.
Here, the world unbends: witness figures
overlapping like clouds, blank with love,
indistinguishable, like the blessed in Heaven.

THE RAPTURE

A green sky, swirling above crowds.
A belief the opening sky would halt.

His gaze could hold it fastened.
A green sky, swirling above crowds.

A door opening into Heaven.
What use is a soul's ascendance?

A door opening into Heaven.
And if my father's stare broke like glass?

The sun is an exit for the sky.
What use is a soul's ascendance?

On the Way to My Father's Death

The plane slips through clouds like a needle through skin.
Cars flicker in and out of focus

along embedded strips of road; minnows
on the river's edge. Lakes turn gold, then lead,

as though we ourselves were revealing the sun
and shading it again. During our descent

I see other planes below us, debating the air.

YOUR SKETCH OF THE CHURCH IN MOURNING

Compare the altar to Rodin's lovers. Hewn
halfway, the surface crosshatched, everything
lies angled, wine and water slanted,
torn bread spilling

fragments on black-veined granite. Draw me
in a stenciled corner of the front row, reluctantly
penciled, smeared to counterpoint
the sharp outlines

of mourners shading other pews. They define the edges
of sorrow; think kohl-tempered eyes or a cobalt necklace.
You hear rising echoes, disembodied
as the thick smell

of your city before a storm. You step with silence,
walking out, and walk slowly. Navigate the marble floor
softly, or you will not hear the dead
call after you.

WALLS

DEDICATORY LETTER

God, your mouth is open. It is an opening
hole, a sincere drop in temperature.

Let me guess: You watched the stock market crumple
like foil, knowing it could be smoothed

with your massive fingernail. These prophetic dreams
always prove false, yet you keep insisting:

bricks will turn to blood, green paint to honey.
Even the underwhelming miracles, such as salt

settling into itself from ocean water,
regularly fail to occur. What happened was that I,

to her, stopped leaving. Now the silkworms
are wrapped tight in their own madness.

Will you hear their cries? Their demands lack teeth.
Their hold on you is an emptied leaf.

God, your eyes are closed, and though your breathing is even
this means nothing. Crops are as easily destroyed

by an apathetic rain as a broken dam.
Still your voice. No one is arguing

imagination is invalid. No one is arguing.
But I believe, with your help, enough will remain.

Your hands are the necessary pages. Let me explain
the myth of the dissident fire.

THE INFLUENCE OF ANXIETY

It weighs more than yesterday, its body
engorged by a grand contradiction, thinning skin
swelled like this breakfast sausage askitter
in the pan. I'm learning over your shoulder
how you bring yourself pleasure, fascinated
at the deftness of your silences, breathing
even held to a fine point. A beautiful girl
is diminished. Somewhere laughter
descends from the highest ceiling to turn
light bulbs into eyes, fans into empty pockets,
and leaves mirrors just as they are. Smells
I praise as ikons of you are stationed around the room.
A pack of seven dogs deceives the street
into being a veldt cracked by drought;
they surround my car with the prolonged slowness
of the starving. They have been emptied
from their leashes, and they weigh more in motion.
Sometimes the sky closes with the peripheral
notion of rain, and you are nowhere to be seen.

DISAPPEARANCES

The darker grass hedging a square pale
from months beneath a disemboweled dryer;
the sealant-blackened stump of a tree limb

sawn off; a question snared
through an accident of acoustics
as we stroll between light-stung buildings:

Where is the sky-washed bar where we met?
Grand Opening signs garnish the buildings,
feed their yawning storefronts. We move confidently

but maybe everything is different in daylight,
the sidewalk bejeweled with silver gum wrappers,
the neon of the bar transfigured to a caramel gray.

From the Honeymoon Album

1

His hand arrested in a wave
or a descent, away from her body—
she is removing herself from the curb
into or over a collection of images
in water. She is floundering in the wind,
her dress hanging back, clinging
to his slacks. There is no way to tell
the depth of the water, or his expression
crowded behind her parade of hair.

2

Light is a veil stretching over them.
Here is half her hand, her face clean
as though love is gone. The floor
is apparent, inside him, setting the bed
like a table. Through the window,
a sign: OPEN ALL. Her eyes are closed.
Her limbs have arranged themselves like cats.

3

Behind them a lamp is hiding
from their faces. Just inside the door
the man concerns her, his lips swollen
in profile, a cancer. There is stillness
except at the light switch where her hand
divides into thin ghosts above, below,
the switch a cage of fingers.

ACROPOLIS

          Buildings hogged the sky that morning
on Studiou, Panepistimiou. They allowed
the Acropolis was a hidden god. We spilled coins
as though casting fortunes, and lost
them among the cobblestones.
                         Your night labored
with dreams of meat, we ate all day
transporting dripping bundles between restaurants,
even to the Acropolis where grease
mixed with clear puddles, where temple bones
held their joints with friezes. The roof was rampant
with the outlines of figures edged between
abandoned limbs.
                 The wind polished the air to glass,
gleaned the distant shore a dark blue hem. From the hilltop
our hotel was a bone in a nest of bones and our balcony,
where we imagined ourselves watching, was a splinter
of red.

BLOOD PERIMETER

I blind the sunset and dim the sky.
Thin my blood to rust.

She loves the broken oysters on the stones, the drying
boneless bodies, the dried slime flaking as rust.

The roads grow holes. The worn asphalt
striates, embracing its own kind of rust.

Learning saltwater is corrosive, the robot
drinks the sea to feel itself refigured to rust.

Cold bleeds into my trailer, creeping
past the sun. I've patched the walls with rust.

STRANGE CHILDREN

You will build a temple, said God through the mouth of Ezra,
and lay the foundation with obedience.

Ezra heard sand slide under a lizard's feet.
And truth, God added.

The words steamed from his mouth and scalded the air.
And do not take strange wives.

Ezra was without water and God's words
scoured his throat like sand.

You will make the mortar from sand; have I not given you sand?
Ezra stumbled from the desert, reciting plagues

he would not remember. The elders asked him about the temple.
Their children, numbering forty thousand, faltered behind.

Ezra shrugged and said,
"These sons of Israel must drink of Him and drown,"

then fell senseless to the ground. He dreamed
of Israel taking strange wives, knowing they must give up marriage

when God lured them to the desert. He dreamed
that strange wives had stranger children.

Ezra collected these children, whose eyes were fevered coals,
and led them to the sea.

BROTHERHOOD

We let the wedding party leave us, my brother
and I, then rushed to what I'd found
behind a wall: a rash of bloody feathers

that led, like a trail of petals, to a hole in the ground.
We rounded the castle to watch blue pare the horizon,
a blue utterly unlike the dirty puddle water I'd drowned

my thirst in, the heat turning my skin and throat to one
seamless husk. There was a sense of order:
we whistled the wild dogs closer, watched them run

down a startled rabbit and huddle, a blush of fur.
Still farther away, we heard one dog's whines
and laughed. It haunted the circle of food. Now I wonder

at that field, all that was hidden by its height, the lines
of grass that caught the wind, bent in the half-light
almost to breaking. Those stalwart kinds

of natural sufferance were fading, but still bright
while dusk drained into the sky. When we heard our mother,
the dog's howls were as worried and as right.

INVADER

*"They will rise," he said. "When the forest is empty
and needs new animals."*
                         –Andrea Barrett, "Birds with No Feet"

The wall is nibbled into opening.

Inside, there is no exit except my entrance, curled in disfavor.

We enter, a multitude of one, and scratch our cryptograms to herald absence.

We enter and scratch our chloroforms.

Plastic coats the teeth, it reinvents the stomach.

Daylight allows exploration; deep echoes coat the darkness.

Less and less motion.

Containers dribble gold to make my steps slick and demonstrative.

In these sanded caves, large enough for a thousand nests, we have each other.

We enter from forgotten tunnels, a furtherance of graves.

I infiltrate stones to find hollows.

There are edges to the sky and fragments to the earth, all glittering sun.

The tracks of some great predator have been erased.

My teeth are sharp.

My teeth are sharp.

I nibble the wall to a close.

LIVING SPACES

QUARANTINE

I've nailed the family into their home.
When the sounds within cease, the entire
will be set on fire. I am always needed
to listen at another door, knock every hour,

address the confessions with silence, accept
the bribes they slide under the door
which I've been instructed to neglect.
But I boil it all, then shrive the piles

under the guidance of a priest who spends
his days dividing prayer from need.
The church doors are locked, but who will blame him
when the proud beaked doctors fall like mustard seeds

on a stone road. The city gates are blessed
with holy chains. My lover lies in her bed
chronicling those who will not last,
who will swell the river, quit uncertainty

with a second, wider smile. It's true
all the alchemists are dead.
As for the rest, I trust my lover's voice
sweet as her body I smell through the wood.

The Alchemist's Genealogy

Rapture. Distilling back into the world
of metal and mineral, our ancestors
beyond the walls of light hear the scrape—

There. Taste. The rough of my father's skin:
charred beef, chicken bones ground to flour.
I've trained my tongue for years to decipher

submerging flesh. This soil, this fine wine
of darkness, occupied by a patient body.
Move trees and their attendant graves into rooms,

Bright October. Remove indecency
from the mulch of mourning clothes
and divide the tangy bite of bone

from the shade of this Paris cemetery.
I'm eating spoonfuls of dirt, the body so long
in that grave the earth alone has enjoyed.

MARY FIGHTS THE MEMORIES OF HER TONGUE

Step 1: inspect a childhood photograph. Light can appear
from nothing. Sunspots push their light somewhere else.
At night, a forest bursts into clarity. The deer go blind.

Step 2: learn juggling and mathematics. Count each revolution
of lemons, limes, olives, and onions. Meditate on division
and distribution. Wade up to your shins in broken fruit.

Step 3: the study of distances. Lip to lip, of course,
and hand to mouth, but also alchemy, which remedies
chemistry. Regarding chlorophyll, light is not the leaf.

Step 4: acceptance of a small gift. You can bereave
and still not be bereft. Cracker Jacks always claim a prize.
Repeat: I am not what I eat, I am not what I eat.

Her Lover, Gone to Buy a Drink, Perhaps

The room says, *Have a drink* in a voice she can't paint over
or strip. She strips layers of her clothing
with each drink, soaking in the cool

remove of the room's gaze.
Her lover would turn up the fan
until the blades lost themselves.

She remembers the ballroom, open
and sweltering, and women spinning
to cool themselves down. The trick is to hold your breath

until he returns or you gasp
for another drink. Cobblestones wink
through a veil of asphalt and a fat man sings his roses

from the corner. The flowers are livid
as welts. The room says, *No.*
But the street. The street. It has unwrinkled in the rain.

The Demonstration

The day before the riot the Gypsy stopped us.
Her Greek was vicious, her open hand steady

as the table where we'd eaten gyros, the meat
freshly slivered from a discolored haunch.

Anna buried her hand in her purse. *She knows
we have bad luck*, by which Anna meant

her first husband. The old woman's teeth
shielded her tongue, but her words took root in the air.

Anna's hands set drachmas like calling cards
onto the Gypsy's palm. *The bad luck's in the money,*

but with it she can cure us. I laughed
even as more bills settled onto her hand

like the pale grey pigeons in the plaza
where the changing of the guards takes place.

SODOM

The Devil had said all the witnesses were dead
but Sodom still smoldered in the distance. Then the cows
appeared, smelling of apples, and walked me home
explaining everything. "Our lot was not
whoring or moneylending, but still we died
when fire ate the sky. Remember this."

THE FUNERAL

He died in the English way, quiet and unassuming.
The car was found arranged by the roadside,

the body inside decorously sprawled, all evidence
of wounds soaked into his black jacket.

One arm politely covered his face. His joints rested
at embarrassed angles. The seatbelt sagged

like a guilty child when the door was pried open,
when ambulance lights lit through unbroken windows

to reflect on the moving hands of his watch.

THE BUTCHER

The counter, the floor, the apron
are all at home in blood.

There is a cut on his wrist
he does not remember making,

and he does not remember how the rain
cleaned the street of people, as a child,

how the water felt warm washing him
free of dirt and now the rain

outside, gathering the scraps of the day
to some slop house miles off

through the ground, the rain so fierce
he asks it in

and holds the guttering pulse on his wrist out
to the crowded air.

MEANINGS

Her eyes are called her hands,
the table is a limestone quarry, this pen
a cubic foot of air, hearts shelled
pecans she cracks.
            In the library she hunts
dust-eaten shelves
for dictionaries. On their ink-fattened pages,
death is the moment
rain hangs in the air.

Her father died a simile.
She burns her grief page by page.

SWORD OF DAMASCUS

We conceive of the world as knowledge, translated
to an atlas. We can know Damascus

and, like him, we inure ourselves to inevitable lies.
We fear death. We fear keyless maps.

At this time, in a motel room, a man fixes a sword
to the ceiling with string and waits.

On the floor beside him are keys that have become themselves,
antecedent to nothing, gaining mass.

Gods are not fickle. The paths they plan
are always inconceivable and meet—

Damascus praised himself and, for that, was changed,
laid out as a roiling land and was built upon.

Sunlight and suicide are irretrievable. Nothing is blank
with meaning. Light reflects us

into being and defines our lack, so we are holy
with light. Define fate: a sentence.

The man in the motel on the bed like a spider
in its web, willing the prey to touch down.

LAST SHOW AT THE SLIP KNOT

The crowd assumes a pose of surprise as he introduces
his tricks, a panoply of self-effacing machines:
a glass vat of briny water, the expected coffin,

a refrigerator large enough for a small man. Nameless
awe is his specialty, creating a wonder
familiar as watching someone die

for the first time or finding a dandelion seed
in the air, hung like a wisp of cloud,
far from any flower bed.

AGORAPHOBIA

Look up and a nutshell carves itself into the sky,
wormholes draining light
like a car dripping oil. Under this coffee-shop roof,

surrounded by glass and the pop
of empty air, concrete is quicksand.
But your hand lies there

like a painted anchor, a string of fishhooks
dulled with wear,
a twin I cannot name, a gag,

a one-way mirror, a mannequin
on a thin lattice of steel, a trellis
for thorns, a cupped nest,

there, on your side of the table, prepared.
A mug steams between us
like a wall merging with air.

THE NAKED TABLE

You said you wanted to sleep with me.
There is a demonstration tonight, and we are strangers

in Athens. We thread streets through garbage
arranged like monuments to a forgotten war.

Gyros sizzle and spit from streetshop windows;
black flies are the city's wandering eyes.

Retsina cleans our tongues with the taste of sleep.
We drink at a naked table. Now the streets

are barren and the café undresses.
It is safe to go home, you say, and guide me in the dark

with fingernails on my back. Your heels click on the cobblestone
like horses' hooves or a soldier's boots.

"Confess," you'd said, asleep

Empty seats surrounded us. At the café
you put your palm to my lips,
said you'd dreamt of Merlin pinned naked

to the round table, a sword through each limb.
The flower beds were edged
with frost that night

I woke to your choked scream.
You flinched away from me. Our windows,
and the ones across the street, were crystallizing.

I confess: In that oblique light
you were growing younger, more beautiful,
your eyes open and unaware.

ELEGY FOR THE END OF THE DAY

Sunlight threads itself through the trees
and in its dusk we are accidents
loving what has run us through.

The table holds a pool of honey
from which our shadows stretch away;

the birds have retreated to their nests,
the feral cats to hollows beneath the house,
but our dog, gold-dipped by the crouching sun,
makes a last circuit of the weed-eaten lot.

He sniffs in starts, lunges to catch an insect
entwined with the slipping light.

When the shadows devour the leaves
I remember your skin, perfect
for vanishing against unlit wood.

Bless this ending, this empty husk
that does not need to be saved.

ALLEYS

NOT A LOVE LETTER

One

The desert sky opens like the mouth of a dying fish.
Night adopts the scent of chlorine. Nothing moves,
though the stars stutter warnings through the clouds—
too much self-martyrdom and though I am all holes
I cannot make myself a saint. I can make myself
a sandwich. I search for the memory of you
but only recall that time I fasted for two weeks,
drinking your name, and soon left no trace in the air.
This desert is the opening parenthesis of sex.
I have heard the jackhammer wind push grain
after grain into a dune. Now, the stilled air
prepares my body for passage into the horizon:
from the moon descends a scratched pillar,
its surface liquid with climbing bodies.
The voice says, *You have lived too long alone.*
Step forward and hang yourself from my side.

Two

Dear to whom it is concerned, you have left
yourself here. In olden days every church
had a portion of its patron reliquaried.
Please find an aspect of your heart enclosed.
Realize, the reflection in the bathroom mirror
of you holding your right breast in your right hand
remains. The devotees are not dissuaded.
Your altar has imprisoned their fingertips.

Three

To want so much. A train wreck.
A line in the geologic records.
Too much, let's retract, say a kitten
unweaned by the side of a river,
thankfully still an excess.

To want so little. The sand trap.
A world vanished by fog. Your voice
saved on a tape, secreted
in a stranger's home, a transcription
in your hands along with the demand.

As you accept my body, note the cost.
Sweat is an even exchange with the air.
With enough belief, you will not drown.
Come, come, your lips are scissors.
At the bottom of the lake we glitter.

The Nuns Remove Their Noses and Lips

It was an heroic instance of virtue in the nuns of a certain abbey,
who cut off their noses and lips to avoid violation....
        –Anna Letitia Barbauld

What did the nuns know
while the brightening abbess
prayed over the paring knife
that wailed against the whetting stone?

The nose is where temptation rests,
the nuns knew that, how it takes root
when conscienceless pheromones
flush the organs with blood.

Silent, the nuns understood lips
were not for speech alone;
but even in eating there is a scent
of pleasure, even in edging their mouths

along the rosary's crucifix.
They were disciplined.
They pursed their lips for a kiss,
offered themselves one by one.

LIMITS TO SCIENCE AND MEDICINE

*In 1822, William Beaumont, a surgeon in the U.S. Army, went to the
Canadian border to treat a 19-year-old trapper hit by a shotgun. The boy
recovered, but he was left with a hole in his abdomen. According to Porter,
Beaumont "took advantage of his patient's unique window" and dropped
food in on a string.*
                                        ~Austin Bunn, "The Bittersweet Science"

In a similar way, with skin flayed back from the chest
and a small alcove revealed for the heart,
track how love is filtered into the body. Can it clot?

If so, how is the barbed knot of it excised
without fixing the hole in the torso? With fingernails,
what divides the instrument from the scientist?

Say *a flock of birds crossing the highway, thousands
of dark arrowheads arrayed against the clouds,
is a suture for the sky.* What does it mean

to be completely understood, to have an eye
that comprehends the inside, that follows the light
digested by the nerve, makes of it a manual for the world?

Hold yourself like a string. Realize what it means
to hold a stone, and that if there were a door
in the stone we could disassemble the hinges.

POET WILL EAT HIMSELF

It is a statement absorbing all questions. Look out
at the darkness beyond the streetlamp. Who undresses
their hands to feel the raw snow while still miles from home?

During an average lifetime enough skin and hair is shed
to create ourselves several times over. Where are these
empty spaces? Who have I stepped away from?

It's too late for breakfast, call it what you will. A treatise
on the life cycle is incomplete if it doesn't say "simple cellulose
can not be absorbed without attendant organisms, without arrangements

of stomachs filtering in sequence." With the cropped grass
come some stunned butterflies, blind from the sun's
sudden eclipse. There is always some beauty to be understood

only through digestion. The body itself is a corporation
of vested self-interests, the bacteria in balance with the blood,
the clotted marrow ending in the tiny blue tongues of veins.

The Skin is Full of Sound

He... won't let go of the skin till it's full of blood.
—Horace

Tom swore off dope when the devil dropped in,
taking a seat on the hood of his truck and somewhat
interfering with his driving, a reaction I felt a bit extreme.
This is why I avoid Georgia. This is why I have given up
long-distance anything. Contrary to popular opinion
this does not make prayer difficult, though it does increase
transportation costs. Some clown cars fit ten, some twenty,
but there isn't one yet built for the single painted fool.
Can a person no longer lie undisturbed like a rotten fruit
without some changeling from the past emerging with starfish
for eyes and a sodden letter condensed in one hand, presented
like Excalibur, this figure spitting teeth as if to say, "No"?
Perhaps that's why we sing in the shower with a muffle
of water though, scientists say, water is a liquid
and so conducts sound more clearly. Rain approaches
like a shroud and, so doing, wraps sunlight in sheets
of cloud, sheets like those my father last lay in,
burned, I hope, to become a tangible ghost.
But can a person no longer lie drunk, half removed
from the tub, face cool on the tile floor still wet
with something I'd have to open my eyes to identify,
right arm pale and immovable without circulation,
a reproving hum in the ear facing the air, a weight
like another body pinning my feet to porcelain? Perhaps
that's why I hear Tom yet reciting Horace, through my ear
on the floor, like the tremors of what will become a tidal wave
still so deep in the ocean there is no betrayal of it on the surface.

TENDING THE FIELD

Small hills interrupt
the field and divine summer
as a hot wasting.

Still, we are paid well
to scour this place of ants
and lay down virgin

sod. With our dark spades
we dig miniature graves
and pile the living

in wheelbarrows, then
repair the field with ripe grass.
We pray to the clouds.

Rain brings worms waving
into view, quick with the need
to breathe. Under skies

threaded with lightning
they explain our just holes and
weave them with their own.

ANOTHER POEM ON RED
after Claire Bateman

The sun a ravaging smear
through eyelids, skin adopting
that perfectly damaged shade:
the red of the distressed
inside of a chicken breast
only partially boiled.
The scarves of ashes left,
the passionless detritus
in the brothel's heatlamp glow,
keep records of what was alive
and, now, blueprints—
like the lines left just above
the ground when the house
I'd abandoned as a child
burnt down—remind us,
in a clinical way, exactly
what has been taken.
And although this may be the first
you've read of it, everything
has a touch of the color,
even if slapped into our cheeks
by our mothers. Those iron columns
inherently designed to rust,
the oxide seducing decay, sad giants
in mourning dress. In ecstasy
the lips puffed with blood,
the wearing away of the painted
disguise and, beneath, that red
a kiss imagined in the dark.
Even the brown sparrows
have a burning ancestor
whose red-copper wings
echo through their feathers
moments before the sun sets.

GOODBYE TO GREECE, GOODBYE TO CYPRUS

A chlorine sky let in a sun without heat.
You stood like an icicle

when the pay phone interrupted,
asking for more. Rumpled tourists

glowed in the fragile atmosphere
while natives walked close to buildings.

This you saw from the hotel balcony, drawing the shades
to keep the view to yourself;

your mouth a thorny rose,
your arms around him vines.

He left like a summer month:
the hotel room half-empty, half-perfect,

you woke to the maid's perfunctory knock.

RECLAMATION
for Meredith

You have fled so far south the cold can only hint
at what you miss: footprints in the sand crisp

as hoofprints in the snow; the emptiness
in the air before a blizzard. What was your test

for the future? Those flowers every year resurrecting
bees from their catacombs and the profligate stink

of honey? Philosophers say we can walk to the past,
again, yes, but we can never reclaim it intact,

so why bother? Idiots. When you've caught a fish
and let it hang in the air, allowed the line to twist

a descent to the boat's deck where it slaps down
like a whip in the dust before a lion, all sound

focuses to the unhooking you correctly perform.
The fish regains completely the water, of course.

PROMISES

Even the flies are smaller. Looking back,
the granite bench adhered to all expectations,
but its surface is scored like limestone,
rock replaced with dirt and gum. Even the skin
of old gods sags, the structure beneath
shrunken and perfect. But this is not enough.
Parts of us are still there, worn into the stone,
a thread of your green skirt, blood
from a scraped knuckle. It's these memories
singing ever deeper. Your face, the slope
of your nose, becomes the rosary that wears
with prayer, that shines with disappearance.

DREAM OF SMALL THINGS

I dream you encased in gold, a museum piece
drawing huge crowds. In the confusion, anyone
can snatch a hand and, already, your eyes are gone.
The hall is distraught with vacant pedestals.

I asked you, What does it mean to be unrhymed?
The expected fortunes without heirs. Your accent
divorced from country, your skin an end in itself.
The straight arm is meaningful only next to the bent.

There is no understanding without rhyme, you said.
And even with it, we inhale enigmas like death and feath-
er, the ibis feather Thoth settles against souls before after-
life begins. All of what we are evolves to metaphor

for weight and, weighed down with unrequited lust,
I will descend. Friend can pair with end, dreams
with seems. I wake and still hope to be awoken.
Although we die, not all bodies rhyme with dust.

You said, For a time very small words kept me alive.
Pictures went blind in your albums. The sea
became an answer, how gold would emerge from saltwater
if we but had the machine. If. And. Was. Will be.

One of the Unburied Dead

Then I will know I am one of the unburied dead,
one of the moving walking stalking talking unburied dead.
                    ~Carl Sandburg, *The People, Yes (#105)*

On this clear day I can be everything.
The clouds reaching down with their folds. The street
studded with stopped cars in both directions.
Knots of people marking bus stops. A brown bird
that skims the sidewalk then quickly slips

into the sky. I lose sight to a rash of offices
and am reminded what we are denied. In planes
cities are specimens splayed out on a slide,
not real as a virus is not real, not in the world.
The world is the abandonment of pretense, some say

desire. Light that falls all that distance
oils the spring leaves transparent. The moon
sometimes interferes with the sky. Closer, a nest
of cicada shells, just out of reach, stirs in the breeze.
My skin splits. The dead are still walking.

EXITS

HIS BODY MAKES ITS WAY HOME

The lion griefs loped from the shade
And on our knees their muzzles laid,
And Death put down his book.
                    —W. H. Auden, "Out on the lawn I lie in bed"

The ground refused his body, so how could we
endure its presence, its arms laid
by its side in a stiff deceit of relaxation.
His coffin was removed by gravediggers
who claimed the burial failed, bad for business.
We would not take the body back
even when the eyelids opened like wounds
with the first rain. We did not relent and lay out
the corpse in his bed, or even store it in the cellar
with the other preserves. A mortician was hired
to keep the body on its grave until it descended
properly. Yet, it managed. Mornings we would find
kind neighbors had deposited it on our porch
and posed it lifelike in the rocking chair.
The morning breeze set it moving.
From our windows we watched joggers wave
and be comforted by the smile from its mouth.

My Mother and My Brother Wake My Father

It is finished. And yet, a thread lingers,
as a caterpillar hangs itself

from a tree, seems to float on light,
the tie too thin to be believed.

Now is when we are most vulnerable.
This anchor yet to be surfaced.

In the Middle Ages people knew devils
to inhabit the dead after devouring

the soul and so stocked candles, always
kept a vigilant someone in the room.

These hours can unwrap the soul
and slip a stranger in its place;

what stalks us when light has done
scattering itself. A cold breath. My family

hovers above the bed, is noticed
like a blink, after it's gone.

(and the air grows more hollow, and the door

THE CREMATION

Fire burns the body, the body burns to air
and rushes from the oven. With a rapturous tick,
heat breathes and becomes aware.

The heat escapes the oven, but goes where?
Drought bleaches the grass. The air fills with static.
Fire burns the body, the body burns to air

which wraps itself in smoke and absorbs our stare.
The dream is aromatic:
heat breathes and becomes aware

of the threatening sky, the clouds dark and bare
with texture. This is the trick:
fire burns the body, the body burns to air

that swirls in the grass and must not care
about its fate both innocent and tragic.
Heat breathes and becomes aware.

It believes it is not tragic, but rare,
and knows now transfiguration is semantic.
Fire burns the body, the body burns to air
heat breathes and becomes aware.

AFTER THE CREMATION

Cradling the urn, I feel the awkwardness
of the bones inside and miss the dissonant

scent of ash. Coffee suffuses the air.
I drink it scalding, as if to label myself alive.

THE CURE AT KRAKÓW

That march of blues like water at the turning over
of the tide, words slipped out like blood
from a refreshed wound. The spider that decorates forever
the pages of the book, its lifeline hanging like a ribbon
from the closed history. Who smells the horseshit
when flowers garnish every doorway? Stones
dress in pigeon feathers. The cats
have ended their centuries-long hunt
and are absent now, having taken all desires
into themselves. Around the corner,
the people echo their laughter from windows.
Cracked open, they still appear closed, the light
from televisions sealing their lives like a veil.
Across the square a statue bends her head.
The tall towers of the churches roll in the wind
as darkness comes, and stars
seem to bring themselves closer
to the man crying over his last meal,
the stench finally unavoidable.

WHAT IS

[W]hat is is what should be.
            —Wallace Stevens, "The Comedian as the Letter C"

Dust sits on every chair and waits
            to be impressed. There is no taint
of mildew yet, but the air is soft
            and thick. Rain runs down the window,
                        and seeps under.

Cobwebs settle in transparent sheets,
            thin but concealing. The spiders
are filling the cracks in the wood floor,
            the vents, the drain, the unlocked door.
                        The clock strikes air.

Was empty ever meant to be? No
            cup was carved for air. Monuments hold
time, as a bed's worn hollow proves us
            there, alive. Ozymandias
                        is gone again.

Do not despair. A desert cannot
            compare to this room, this vast suite,
this mansion sheathed in bare white plaster
            and tile, where all surfaces stare.
                        Distant. Aware.

The sun breaks the ground into rough swaths
            of brown and green. Shadows crawl through
morning like minks, their frayed edges taut,
            dreaming of reflections to eat
                        with oily teeth.

CHRISTMAS DAY, ST. PETER'S SQUARE

The air so thick with breath it is like Heaven.
And there, beneath
the upraised hands clenching medallions

on this day of blessing, my father,
small in the crowd, holds a sun-polished medal on a chain
before his eyes, consults the twirling metal

like a compass.
On it the patrician smile of a pope,
who says, "Remember me as this wafer of bronze.

Darkness will blush my face
and even my eyes
will fade to blank weight on your chest."

TOO STEEP TO CLIMB

In the air the still distant and uproarious smoke
scaling the dark rungs of trees to unwind
into twists of small shadow eaten by the clouds.
The crematorium is just one thin spoke

of ritual holding us at bay, and what a kind
dictator to present death only as a shroud.
Forgive me, father, for I have missed
your skin, your eyes, I have been blind

to your absence. Sometimes as I've drowsed
an insistent voice (I've called it yours) has kissed
my ears ungently and scoured me from sleep
hungry for more. We were left a crowd

of ashes and bone. I've tried to make a list
of what was lost. I want to say however much I keep.
Take this one answer: life is the dawn and our souls,
if that is who we are, are burned from the earth like mist.

Be comforted. There is no grave so deep
it does not fold again into a mountain.

WALKING FROM THE FUNERAL

People cordon themselves under eaves
while curbside drains clog with leafy bouquets

awkwardly fluttering in shallow lakes.
Rain fills your walk with seductive chatter.

Three lightning bolts divide the sky
and bow to the night. A fallen branch

lies shivering in the breeze
like a gift on your doorstep.

About The Author

Andrew Kozma holds a B.A. from The George Washington University, an M.F.A from the University of Florida, and a Ph.D. from the University of Houston. Though raised mostly in Virginia and currently living in Houston, he plans on moving to Poland for at least a short while.